BE AMAZING WITH YOUR MONEY

Simple Habits, Hard-Earned Lessons, and Everyday Tips to Build Financial Confidence

LaShon Fryer

This Amazing Money Story is being written by

Your previous money story had co-authors.

This one is being written solo, with clarity and confidence.

WELCOME TO
BE AMAZING WITH YOUR MONEY

Simple Habits, Hard-Earned Lessons,
and Everyday Tips to Build Financial Confidence

If you've ever felt overwhelmed, scared, or just plain unsure about money, you're in the right place. I created this workbook because I've been there, standing at the intersection of "I want better" and "I don't know where to start."

My financial journey wasn't smooth. I made plenty of mistakes, learned the hard way, and survived two financial rock bottoms — once after a failed relationship, and once after the 2008 recession. I know what it feels like to pay all your bills, protect your "four walls" (housing, transportation, food, and utilities), and still feel broke both financially and mentally.

That's why this workbook is much more than just another financial literacy tool. It's built from real-life experiences and a genuine understanding of the challenges many of us encounter when trying to rewrite our money stories. This workbook aims to ease your worries about finances, nurture confidence in your financial choices, and guide you to take small but meaningful steps that can lead to significant achievements over time.

And no, you don't have to have it all figured out. You just have to start — and I promise you, if you commit to changing your financial life, you will change your financial life.

BEFORE YOU BEGIN

Before we dive into building your financial courage, I want you to relax. Take a few deep breaths.

You are not behind.

You are not alone.

And you are not too far gone to change your story.

> **Money isn't just about numbers — it's about mindset.**

If you're feeling anxious, confused, or even a little ashamed about your financial situation, breathe easy.

> **You are not broken — you're just at the beginning of your new chapter.**

I created this project because I lived it. After going through bankruptcy, rebuilding after recessions, and surviving seasons of living paycheck to paycheck, I learned that financia peace starts *inside* before it ever shows up in your bank account.

You'll learn practical money skills here — how credit really works, why you even need credit, how to budget, how to save — but more importantly, you'll build, or rebuild, your financial confidence.

This workbook will help you rewrite your money story, one courageous decision at a time. You don't have to be fearless to change your financial life. You just have to be willing to move forward, even while you're still a little scared.

If you're serious about changing your financial future, this workbook can help — but it starts with you. You'll need a plan, not just hope. A willingness to explore new ideas, even if they feel uncomfortable at first. You'll need to believe in your ability to grow, even when it's hard. You'll need commitment, not perfection. And most of all, an open mind to keep learning.

The tools are here. The guidance is here. But what you get from this is completely up to you. In the end, it's not you versus your credit score — it's you versus the version of you say you want to become.

Now, let's begin this new chapter.

CONTENTS

SECTION ONE

THE START

Your current situation doesn't define your future.

Chapter 1

This is a Very Worn Path— You're Just at the Beginning of It

Understanding the Impact of Survival Mode on Your Peace and Physical Health

Many financial mistakes and mishaps stem from some form of survival mode. When faced with a financial crisis, it is challenging to make rational decisions. When you find yourself "in it," you become fixated on resolving the immediate crisis at hand.

It's very common to make impulsive financial decisions during these times. For example, imagine your car breaks down unexpectedly. You depend on it to get to work, but the only money you have available is designated for rent. In that situation, your priority becomes clear: you need to fix the car. Yes, rent is due in four days, but you still decide to use some or all of the rent to repair your car. If you cannot get to work, you cannot make money. Problem solved.

While you successfully solved that immediate crisis, you likely created another one.

Late rent payments can lead to stress about catching up, incurring fees, or even borrowing more money just to stay afloat. This cycle is familiar to many of us and is easy to fall into, even when we do our best.

It's important to note that survival mode isn't inherently negative; it is often a necessary response to urgent and pressing problems. However, consistently living in this state can lead to profound consequences, not only financially, but also physically and mentally. Research has discovered that prolonged financial stress can lead to serious health risks and conditions such as heart disease, hypertension, as well as mental health issues like depression and anxiety.

Constant worry can take a toll over time, increasing the risk of substance abuse and chronic fatigue. This can make even simple decision-making increasingly difficult. A recent Pew Research Center report showed that "worries related to financial security and personal health are related to higher levels of psychological distress."

And if that's not enough, there is also the worry associated with the long-term hardships of financial stressors, such as:

- Poor credit ratings, which can limit access to loans and housing

- Increased interest rates on any debts, creating a heavier financial burden

- Fewer career opportunities, as financial instability may prevent you from investing in education

Be Amazing With Your Money

or training

- -Ongoing emotional and physical strain that affects overall well-being and quality of life

While short-term survival choices—like paying a bill late or using a credit card to cover essential expenses—may seem like viable solutions at the time, they often add significant weight to your future financial situation.

Over time, these choices can limit your opportunities and create a cycle of stress that becomes more challenging to escape. Recognizing and addressing the underlying causes of survival mode is essential for breaking this cycle and fostering a healthier relationship with money. So, instead of merely surviving, let's acquire the financial tools to thrive.

Chapter 2
Your Mindset

You need to get to the root of the problem to get out of money-related survival mode. I ultimately discovered that my money problems had little to do with my finances or survival and everything to do with my mindset.

Our mindset is the established set of attitudes we possess towards something. Those thoughts and feelings developed unconsciously through our experiences over time. Now, don't get me wrong. Survival mode certainly contributed to my financial ruin, but most of it was more related to my mindset, my mood, and my habits.

Our thoughts are extremely powerful, affecting our minds and financial lives, so we must do something different to get a different result. You will never be able to change what you do not confront. That's why this journey starts here: with your mind.

Changing your mindset and your financial life must be unique to YOU, so we will begin this chapter with a little self-awareness exercise.

A Financial Selfie

This self-assessment is your financial moment of clarity—no edits, just insight and awareness. It is a snapshot of where you really are financially, emotionally, and mentally. Take your time and answer honestly. Nobody else needs to see this but you.

Step One: Reflect

1. Do you spend money to fill an emotional void? (Example: Do you shop or fill your virtual cart online to cheer yourself up or relieve stress?)

2. Do you live paycheck-to-paycheck?

   - If yes, is it because you don't earn enough at your current job?

   - Or because you're living above your means?

3. Do you know your current financial situation?

   - Do you regularly check your bank statements, pay stubs, or credit card balances?

4. Do you know exactly how much money comes in and how much goes out each month?

FYI:

It's completely natural to feel uncertain about some of your responses at this stage. Lean into it as an opportunity for growth, which allows you to craft a better story that is uniquely yours. Believing in yourself should start at this stage as well. The next section will outline a few actions you can take immediately to build financial confidence.

Small Shifts That Lead to Big Changes

Below are some practical things you can start doing today:

- If you are an emotional spender, ask yourself, "Do I really need this, or do I just want it?" If it is not necessary, do not buy it. Consider waiting 24 hours before making non-essential purchases. This will give you time to check in with your feelings first.

- Living paycheck-to-paycheck because of low income? Consider applying for a higher-paying job, learning a new skill, or starting a side hustle. (Your gift will make room for you.)

- Are you avoiding the truth? Open those statements. Track your spending and create a simple budget. Set aside 15–30 minutes weekly to check your finances.

Step Two: Train Your Mind Like a Muscle

- Be intentional about what you consume. Just like you can't eat junk food every day and expect good health, you can't flood your mind with negativity and expect peace.

- Nurture your goals. You don't need to know someone personally to be mentored by them. Read their books. Watch their interviews. Study their stories — and you'll realize yours isn't that different. (There is a list of phenomenal books in the resources that should be available for free to check out at your local library.)

- Protect your peace. Change is uncomfortable, and you will face challenges. Whether prayer, meditation, music, movement, or talking to someone who understands you, identify what helps you reset and return to it often. (If that doesn't work, find me online somewhere.)

- Understand your motivation. You need to know why you're making this change. On tough days, your "why" will sustain you when your willpower struggles. (More on this in a later chapter)

- Start acting like you have already achieved your goal. Believe it. Speak it. Move like it. Transformation starts in the mind first. That's why we begin here.

Financial Reflection

What's one small step I'm willing to take this week — even if it feels scary?

_____

_____

_____

_____

_____

What do I need to stop doing to get closer to the financial life I want?

_____

_____

_____

_____

_____

_____

Chapter 3
Your Money Story—
Rewriting the Script

With over 347 million people in the United States, nearly everyone interacts with money daily. Yet, conversations about money often stir a range of emotions. For some, money discussions evoke joy and prosperity; for others, they trigger stress and discomfort. These reactions are deeply rooted in our individual experiences and mindsets.

> Our mindset shapes how we perceive and handle money. From childhood to adulthood, our financial behaviors are influenced by the narratives we've internalized.

Growing up, I believed that financial struggle was the norm. My family often grappled with meeting basic needs, and the idea of a paycheck lasting until the next payday seemed like a luxury reserved for others. Without exposure to financial literacy or positive money management examples, I lacked a healthy relationship with money.

But here's what's interesting: both my maternal and paternal grandparents actually had exceptional credit, savings, and even owned multiple rental properties. In fact, they were the ones my parents would turn to when robbing Peter to pay Paul—still did not cover our monthly living expenses.

As a child watching this play out, I unknowingly absorbed the belief that having good credit and "extra" money was something that only came with older age and wisdom— that you had to struggle first and succeed much later. Only part of that turned out to be true. Quite honestly, I didn't respect money because I felt it didn't respect me. But as I learned later, respect begets respect.

Understanding your financial past is the first step toward building a healthier financia future.

Your Current Money Story

This exercise is about self-reflection. There are no right or wrong answers, so be honest and write in your own words. The goal is to examine your current relationship with money and identify narratives that may need reshaping.

1. What is your earliest memory about money?

2. What was your favorite money-related memory growing up?

3. What was your worst money-related memory growing up?

4. Compared to your peers, did you have more, just enough, or less?

5. How were money conversations handled in your household?

6. What emotion do you associate with money today?

7. How do you feel about saving money?

8. What are your thoughts on giving money away?

9. Complete the sentence: Money is. _____

10. What one word describes your childhood money memories?

11. How would you describe your parents' relationship with money?

12. What lessons did your parents teach you about money?

13. Can you identify any recurring themes in your financial experiences?

14. How have these experiences influenced your current financial situation?

Insights from *The Psychology of Money* by Morgan Housel

Morgan Housel emphasizes that our personal experiences heavily influence our financia decisions:

> "Your personal experiences with money make up maybe 0.00000001% of what's happened in the world, but maybe 80% of how you think the world works."

This highlights the importance of understanding and, if necessary, reshaping our money narratives.

Writing Your New Money Story

Various factors and people have influenced your initial money story. Now is the time to take control and create a narrative that aligns with your current values and goals.

Before you start, however, remember to extend some financial grace to yourself and consider the following:

- Acknowledge past mistakes without judgment.

- Define Your Financial 'Why': Identify what motivates you—whether it's supporting family, purchasing a home, starting a business, or achieving financial independence.

- Educate Yourself: Knowledge is power.

- If you're feeling stuck, consider reading a book or a few chapters from the recommended materials in the resource section.

- Be sure to include small, achievable goals in your new narrative about money.

- Take practical steps such as using coupons, paying bills early, or investing in quality over quantity.

Remember, rewriting your money story is a journey; don't worry, there is no deadline. Do not feel as if you need to censor yourself, and do not worry about using perfect grammar or being an expert on financial jargon. Write your money story in your language since it is strictly for you. The primary goal of writing your money story is for you to identify the relationship you want with your money and your finances. Be sure to include celebrations for **even the smallest of victories, stay committed, and know that each step brings you closer to financial well-being.**

_____

_____

_____

_____

_____

_____

_____

_____

_____

_____

_____

_____

Chapter 4
Poverty Mindset
Vs.
Prosperity Mindset

"Do not believe everything you think." —

Byron Katie

Transforming your financial journey begins with a change in mindset. While many of us understand this, it's common to overlook that deciding to change is just the starting point. The real challenge comes with the ongoing commitment needed to turn that decision into reality. Embracing this journey can be difficult at times, but with consistency and dedication, the rewards can truly be life-changing.

I only started making progress with my finances when I adopted a better decision-making process. I previously approached my money with a poverty mindset, and I had not learned everything I needed to unlearn yet.

Regardless of your age, you likely have realized that you need to unlearn certain beliefs and habits—or perhaps you've already begun that process.

At the beginning of my journey, there were plenty of instances when, despite earning a decent salary and having money in the bank, I still made several poor financial decisions. I would spend much more than necessary on brand-new cars—not because I genuinely wanted that make or model, but to impress other people. I also wasted ridiculous amount of money on the latest trends, even when I didn't like some of them.

Financial sidebar: Just because a particular brand costs a lot of money does not mean it is *worth* a lot of money. For example, I love Nike, but if you dry some of their cotton items, get ready to give them away. This isn't to say some of their products aren't made well, and the Nike Pegasus is not my go-to gym shoe every time, but their tees and sweats? Air-dry only if you intend to wear them again.

When we buy luxury brands such as Gucci, Louis Vuitton, Dior, etc., we're not just paying for the materials and construction but also investing in prestige, exclusivity, and a unique experience. The difference between production costs and retail prices can be unbelievable, with markups ranging from 50% to an astonishing 3000%. This means that when you choose a luxury item, you're embracing more than just a product; you're participating in a lifestyle that embodies sophistication and status.

Research suggests that a poverty—or scarcity—mindset drives behaviors focused not just on competition but also on hoarding and self-preservation. Another sign of a poverty mindset is spending your money as fast as you earn it, just to return to what's familiar— being broke. On the other extreme, some people with a poverty mindset will hoard every penny they make out of fear of losing it. Both responses come from fear, and both can be damaging.

When you fear you won't have enough money to meet your obligations, you are expressing a persistent belief that economic resources are limited. According to research published in *Science* (2013), scarcity reduces mental bandwidth and decision-making power, which can lead to a cycle of poor financial choices.

Even though I was never destitute, I still operated with a poverty mindset because I hadn't edited my money story yet. My grandparents would have said I was "competing with the Joneses." You may be too young to have heard that phrase before, but I'm sure you've seen the behavior it describes.

Many of these habits were formed over years of repetition, so unlearning them and correcting those financial mistakes took me some time. You should expect it to take you some time as well. Be patient with yourself and remember to offer yourself grace during this journey.

As stated earlier, our mindsets are shaped by our unique experiences. So, until you intentionally create new experiences, you'll keep repeating the old ones.

To move forward, you must focus more on what's possible and less on what's not. That starts with the way you talk to yourself. The following exercises will help you practice unlearning scarcity-based language and replace it with thoughts supporting a prosperous, confident financial future.

Exercise: Shifting From Fearful to Fearless Financial Language

Instructions: Rewrite the following fear-based statements related to finances into fearless, positive, and prosperous ones.

Fearful Thought	Fearless Thought
I'm bad with money.	I'm learning to manage my money better every day.
I don't have enough money to save.	I can start small. Even if I only save $5 a week, I'll have $20 more than I do now.
I'll never have good credit.	I can improve my credit each month with new financial behaviors.
I'll never make enough money to repay my debt.	Every small payment leads to big results.

Now you try:

Write two or three statements specific to your situation and reframe them.

_____

_____

_____

_____

_____

_____

Practice Unlearning in Your Everyday Life

Sometimes, the stories we tell ourselves have nothing to do with money, but everything to do with how we view ourselves. If you want to grow more confident in any area of life, it starts with changing your language.

Instructions: Rewrite the limiting thoughts below into ones that empower you to keep growing. This exercise will help you build a more positive and prosperous mindset.

Limiting Thought	Limitless Reframe
I'm not good at this.	I'm still learning, and that's okay.
I always mess things up.	I've made mistakes, but I learn from them.
I'll never get it right.	I haven't gotten it right _yet_.
I'm too behind to catch up.	It's never too late to start where I am.
I hate asking for help.	Asking for help is a strength, not a weakness.

Your turn: What are 2–3 things you often say to yourself that might be holding you back? Rewrite them below in a way that helps you feel hopeful and not hopeless.

_____

_____

_____

_____

_____

_____

_____

_____

_____

_____

_____

_____

Chapter 5
What is Your Why?
Because You May Need
to Borrow from It

"He who has a why can endure any how."

Friedrich Nietzsche

Understanding your financial "why" is vital, but it is equally important to know your everyday "why." It's essential to identify the reasons behind your most significant life decisions. Your "why" should serve as your strongest motivator and supporting anchor, especially when life feels overwhelming and you're searching for a reason to keep pushing forward.

In the last chapter, we discussed unlearning certain habits and dropping limiting language because they also limit you. Your "why" will motivate you on those frustrating days when you question if all of this work is even worth it. The purpose behind your why gives you the courage to face the disappointment that often follows a "No." Trust me— you will hear "No" more often than "Yes." However, when you know your why, you will have the fuel to push past those obstacles until you reach your opportunities.

Your why doesn't just lift you up on hard days—it also reminds you that this is bigger than you. When you know exactly why you are doing something, you'll figure out how to do it. Your why creates resourcefulness and resilience. And here's something most people forget: your why can change. It evolves with you. Our whys shift as our priorities and circumstances change.

In his book *Start with Why*, Simon Sinek says,

> **"Working hard for something we do not care about is called stress; working hard for something we love is called passion."**

Right now, my biggest whys are my granddaughters. They're worth the research, the reading one to two books a week, taking courses, working a day job while running a small business, and losing sleep. Before them, my why was my son. I needed creditworthiness to provide a better life for him. And before I had a child, my why was my peace, which gave me the strength to leave relationships, friendships, and even kinships that no longer served me. At the core of all my whys is one constant: service.

Defining your why can be challenging, but it's one of the first steps toward achieving any goal. If you are having trouble identifying your financial why or your everyday why, or maybe you just need to reassess your why, this chapter and the questions below will help you think it through.

Because here's the truth: Change is constant and necessary, but it can also be uncomfortable and exhausting. There are days when my life's work is just as mentally draining as manual labor. And I also know that I'm not the only one who feels that way. I am sure some part of that is true for you as well. On Thursdays (without fail), my grace runs low. My motivation disappears. But instead of quitting, I borrow some energy from my why, or I complete a task that doesn't take too much mental fortitude.

You will likely have some days like that as well, but your why must be bigger than the burden of the work, and it also helps when you have unconditional love for your why.

If you already know your why, that's fantastic. You can bypass this section. However, if you aren't, the why exercise consists of two parts. Your financial why might be closely related to your everyday why, but I believe it's important to distinguish between them. Therefore, let's start with the basics:

What is your motivation for wanting to get your financial life in order? (This should be straightforward because you likely addressed this question when writing your new money story.)

Now, if you are struggling with your everyday why, here are some questions to help you discover—or redefine—your why:

- What kinds of support or advice do people often seek from you?

- What comes easily to you that others find difficult?

- What are you naturally good at?

- How could you use that gift or talent to solve problems—for yourself or others?

- You do a great job teaching people _____

- What is the first thing you would pursue if money didn't matter?

- When you feel at your best, what activities are you engaged in?

- What is one recent achievement that felt meaningful to you?

- You are happiest when. _____

- What problem in the world—or in your own life—won't leave you alone?

- What breaks your heart or stirs something deep inside you?

- Has your why changed in the last few years? If so, how?

- Are you holding onto a why that no longer fits this season of your life?

- Who or what needs you now, and how does that shift your why?

- When you feel defeated, who or what makes it worth trying again?

- Think about whatever made you pick up this workbook. Is it still one of the first things you think about each morning?

Your why is allowed to grow with you, so don't be surprised if it changes by the end of this workbook. That's not a setback—it's growth.

It doesn't have to be perfect, but it does need to be honest. When the work gets hard (and it will), you'll need to draw from it—and if your why is rooted in truth, there will always be enough to pull from.

If you journal:

Write about a time when your why gave you the strength to keep going. What were you facing? How did it feel to be that clear and focused? What do you need today to reconnect with that version of yourself?

_____

_____

_____

_____

_____

_____

_____

_____

_____

SECTION TWO

THE SHIFT

Small Steps Can Lead to Big Changes

Chapter 6

Balling on a Budget
(Without Feeling Broke All the Time)

"A budget is telling your money where to go instead of wondering where it went."

Dave Ramsey

Budget: a plan to help you manage your money.

A budget is the root of financial awareness. It is a tool to help you identify how much money comes in, how much goes out, and how much you can save. Most importantly, it reveals what is important to you.

Fair warning, when you first start budgeting, you may be surprised to discover what you've been prioritizing (or was that just me?). At any rate, once budgeting becomes routine, it's a great way to prioritize your needs, wants, and savings.

A budget is the bridge you will use to reach your financial goals.

According to a 2024 NerdWallet study, 84% of Americans who budget say it helps them feel more in control of their finances. A budget is the best way to control your money before it starts controlling you. It's not just about tracking every dollar — it's about being clear on your values, goals, and what you're willing (or not willing) to sacrifice. By assessing your monthly expenses, you can evaluate your spending behavior, determine where you can cut costs, and redirect funds to where they matter most.

Your budget will help you separate your financial wins from your financial setbacks. Tracking your expenses is the best way to ensure you live below your means instead of pretending like you do.

Now, complete transparency: I absolutely hate doing my budget each month. Yes, I have an MBA and I'm a certified financial coach. I even manage a team and oversee a budget nearing three million dollars annually in my professional life. Yet, despite all that expertise, I still dread those 30 to 60 minutes every month when I must confront my own personal budget.

Many of us know this struggle too well. Why? It makes you feel vulnerable, makes you examine your choices, and can feel restrictive, and nobody wants to be told what to do, not even by their own inner voice. But that changed when I reframed the narrative. Instead of seeing a budget as a limitation, I started seeing it as a plan—*my* plan—to reach *my* financial goals.

It still took me a couple of years to consistently stick with a physical budget. I assumed that I could get away with a *mental budget* because I had financial discipline. I thought I had it handled in my head. Spoiler alert: I didn't.

I forgot expenses, overlooked impulse buys, and became frustrated when my mental balances did not equal my actual balances. To protect my peace and progress, I made budgeting a non-negotiable monthly routine.

Think of budgeting like working out. Most of us don't love it, but we do it because we love the results. We want strength, stamina, and growth. Budgeting is the same — you don't have to love the process, but you will love the peace of mind it brings.

Although budgeting is necessary, it doesn't have to be complicated.

The ideal budget is one you can consistently follow. I like to maintain a simple and smooth process. Fun fact: We do not want to do things that don't interest us, so make it a interesting as possible.

In the past, I used budgeting apps like Every Dollar (a Dave Ramsey favorite — easy to use and free), and now I use an Excel sheet because it fits seamlessly into my routine. Others I know swear by a good old-fashioned pen and notebook.

There's no "right" way to do this. There's only what works best for you. Find a budgeting style that fits seamlessly into the pace of your real life. Choose the method you will most likely stay consistent with, even when life gets hectic.

> "You can't reach your financial goals if you're too afraid to look at your numbers."

On the next page, you'll find a simple budgeting worksheet to get you started and some common budgeting strategies to try. However, if you would like to take the virtual route, here's a short list of free budgeting apps worth trying:

- **EveryDollar**: Super easy to use and free. Ideal for zero-based budgeting.

- **Mint**: Great for monitoring spending and creating savings goals.

- **Goodbudget**: Digital envelope system for people who like to plan ahead.

- **Rocket Money**: Especially helpful for subscription tracking and canceling.

Budgeting Worksheet

Income

Primary Income: $ _____

Secondary Income: $ _____

Other Income (e.g., side gigs, investments): $ _____

Total Monthly Income: $ _____

Fixed Expenses

Rent/Mortgage: $ _____

Utilities (electricity, water, gas): $ _____

Internet/Phone: $ _____

Insurance (health, auto, etc.): $ _____

Debt Payments (loans, credit cards): $ _____

Total Fixed Expenses: $ _____

Variable Expenses

Groceries: $ _____

Transportation (fuel, public transit): $ _____

Dining Out: $ _____

Entertainment: $ _____

Personal Care (clothing, grooming): $ _____

Miscellaneous: $ _____

Total Variable Expenses: $ _____

Savings & Investments

Emergency Fund: $ _____

Retirement Contributions: $ _____

Other Savings Goals (vacation, education): $ _____

Total Savings & Investments: $ _____

Summary

Total Income: $ _____

Total Expenses (Fixed + Variable): $ _____

Total Savings & Investments: $ _____

Remaining Balance: $ _____

Note: The budget worksheet helps you clearly see your monthly finances. Adjust categories as needed to fit your lifestyle. A positive remaining balance indicates a surplus, which can be allocated to savings or debt repayment. A negative balance suggests a need to adjust expenses.

Common Budgeting Strategies

Selecting a budgeting method that aligns with your financial goals and lifestyle is important. Here are some popular strategies:

50/30/20 Rule

- **50%** for Needs: Essentials like housing, utilities, and groceries.

- **30%** for Wants: Non-essentials like dining out, entertainment.

- **20%** for Savings: Emergency fund, retirement, debt repayment.

Zero-Based Budgeting

Assign every dollar of your income to specific expenses or savings goals, ensuring your income minus expenditures equals zero. This method promotes intentional spending.

Envelope System

Allocate cash for different spending categories into envelopes. Once an envelope is empty, no further spending is allowed in that category for the month. This tactile method can curb overspending.

Pay Yourself First

Prioritize savings by setting aside a predetermined amount from each paycheck before addressing other expenses. This approach ensures consistent savings growth.

75/15/10 Rule

- **75%** for Daily Needs: Rent, groceries, transportation.

- **15%** for Long-Term Investments: Retirement accounts, education funds.

- **10%** for Short-Term Savings: Emergency fund, short-term goals.

This method offers flexibility while promoting savings.

Chapter 7
Financial Stories Have a Plot Twist—
Be Prepared for Yours

"You can plan a pretty picnic, but you can't predict the weather"

Outkast

Have you ever had a month when everything was going fine, and then... boom—your car breaks down, your kid gets sick, or your water heater decides it wants to be cold?

That, my friend, is what I call a **plot twist**. The kind you *wish* you could edit out of your real life. But unfortunately, that's not how it works. And if we want to finish this journey strong (and less stressed), we've got to start expecting the unexpected.

This chapter isn't about fear. It's about freedom. It's about building a little safety net so that the next time life starts to life, you are ready.

But first...the real plot twist

According to a Federal Reserve study, nearly 40% of Americans would struggle to cover an unexpected $400 expense. Let that sink in for a few seconds.

That's not about being irresponsible. That's about being overwhelmed. Inflation is real. Rent is real. Groceries? Don't get me started. But this number isn't here to shame you, but to remind you that you're not alone if this is your current story. And more importantly, it's here to show you why having an emergency fund, or what I like to call a "**Plot Twist Fund**," matters now more than ever. Even financial educators like Tiffany "The Budgetnista" Aliche, one of my favorites, emphasize this same idea: *"Small steps add up."* And she's right—saving something, even just $5 a week, is better than saving nothing.

Why most emergency funds feel overwhelming

Most of us hear the words "emergency fund" and think we need to have $1,000 in the bank by the end of the week. That kind of pressure can make anyone shut down, but behavioral science tells us something different.

When we gamify our goals—by turning savings into a challenge, a habit, or a trackable win—we're more likely to stick with them. So, let's break this down in a way that feels achievable instead of draining, and look at some simple ways to seamlessly incorporate saving into your everyday life.

Challenge #1: $25 Paycheck Protection Plan

Every week you get paid, deposit $25 (or more if you can) into your Plot Twist Fund. Set it on autopilot so you don't have to think about it. In two months, you'll have $200 saved without breaking a sweat.

Why it works: Automating takes out the guesswork. No mental math, no excuses.

Challenge #2: 21-Day $1 Day Deposit

Every day for 21 days, set aside $1. That's it. Put that dollar away, whether it's spare change, a roundup from your bank card, or skipped vending machine snacks. Use a jar, a savings app, or even an envelope.

Why it works: It creates a tiny but powerful habit. Plus, it builds momentum.

Challenge #3: 5-for-5 Savings Challenge

Set a timer for 5 minutes. Look around your house for anything you don't use, need, or wear anymore. Then, sell those five items online, at work, or with friends/family. Take the money you make and transfer it directly into your Plot Twist Fund.

Why it works: It's fast, simple, and frees up space while making you cash.

Challenge #4: The Plot Twist Jar

Every time something goes *right* unexpectedly—a free lunch, a canceled appointment, an early dismissal at work—treat that like a "plot twist blessing." Drop $5–$10 in a jar. It'll add up faster than you think.

Why it works: It builds gratitude while building your safety net.

The goal isn't perfection—it's preparation.

You aren't required to complete all four challenges, nor do you have to tackle any of the ones I suggested. Begin with the one that aligns with your finances and can easily fit into your everyday life. Choose the option that suits your lifestyle and give it a try.

Ultimately, **your future self will app**reciate every dollar you save today.

Think of your Plot Twist Fund as your personal bodyguard—quiet in the background, but ready when life tries to swing. And when the next unexpected expense shows up, you won't have to panic because you will be peacefully prepared.

> **Understand the power of saving — even $5 at a time.**
>
> **You can find even more savings challenges on my website:**
> Amazingchapters.com

Chapter 8
Credit Clarity

| "Your credit score doesn't tell your whole story—but it can help you rewrite the next chapter."

L et's start with the truth: credit doesn't define your worth but reflects your current financial behavior. And behavior can be changed.

Don't worry if you don't have a high score yet. Most of us start with little to no credit history, or we've made some money mistakes along the way. The good news? You can build, rebuild, and protect your credit starting today.

I know this personally. Even though I have excellent credit now, my score was once as low as 450 following a relationship breakdown. Financial abuse is a real thing (but that's a story for another day). It took time, strategy, and a lot of patience, but I turned it around. And if I can do it, so can you.

What is Credit?

Credit is a contractual agreement between a borrower and a lender where the borrower receives something of value and agrees to pay for it later under specific terms. When a lender considers offering you credit, they typically check your FICO score to determine how trustworthy—or creditworthy—you are.

Think of your FICO score like your financial GPA. A three-digit number ranging from 300 to 850 gives lenders a snapshot of how well you manage borrowed money. And just like a GPA, it's unique to you and can consistently improve over time.

Here's how FICO scores are generally classified:

- **Poor credit:** 300–579
- **Fair credit:** 580–669
- **Good credit:** 670–739
- **Very good credit:** 740–799
- **Exceptional credit:** 800–850

How Your FICO Score is Calculated

There are five major categories that go into calculating your FICO score:

- **Payment history – 35%**

- **Amounts owed (credit utilization) – 30%**

- **Length of credit history – 15%**

- **Credit mix – 10%**

- **New credit inquiries – 10%**

You may find that not all of these apply to you right now, and that's okay. Let's walk through each one so you know where to focus.

Payment History (35%)

This is the biggest part of your score. Lenders want to know if you pay your bills on time. Late or missed payments can lower your score, but paying consistently—even the minimum—helps build trust.

Amounts Owed (30%)

This is also known as your credit utilization ratio. If you have a credit card with a $2,000 limit and you've used $1,000, your utilization is 50%. Lenders prefer this number to be **under 30%**, and the lower, the better.

Credit History (15%)

The older your credit accounts, the better. A long history of responsible credit use can increase your score. If you're new to credit, that's okay—but opening a lot of accounts quickly can be a red flag.

Credit Mix (10%)

Lenders like to see that you can manage different types of credit, such as credit cards, car loans, student loans, or store accounts. Don't worry if you don't have a mix yet—just build one intentionally over time.

New Credit/Inquiries (10%)

Each time you apply for credit, it appears as an "inquiry." Too many in a short time can hurt your score, so space them out if possible.

The Big Three: National Credit Bureaus

There are three major credit reporting bureaus: **TransUnion, Equifax, and Experian**. These agencies collect data about your credit behavior and use it to create your credit report. Lenders, landlords, and even employers may request your credit report to help them make decisions.

You're entitled to **one free credit report each year** from each of the three bureaus. Visit AnnualCreditReport.com to access yours safely.

Did You Know? You can increase your credit score without taking on more debt, just by paying on time and keeping balances low.

Yes, YOU Can Build Good Credit

If your credit score isn't where you want it to be, don't panic. You are not stuck. Improving your credit is all about progress over perfection. Here's where to start:

- Make on-time payments, even if it's just the minimum.

- Keep your balances low, below 30% of your credit limit.

- Avoid applying for lots of new credit at once.

- Check your credit reports annually to ensure accuracy.

  > **"Credit is not about how much you have—it's how well you manage what you have."**

You've got this. Start small, stay consistent, and remember: your credit score is just one chapter in your financial story. And you can rewrite it however you choose.

Additional Resources:

- My FICO Score

- What Is a Good FICO Score?

- Credit Score Ranges

- How Credit Bureaus Collect Your Data

- Free Annual Credit Report

Chapter 9

Understanding Your Credit Report

Your credit report is more than just a document—it's your financial footprint. It reflects your credit history and plays a pivotal role in determining your financial opportunities. Regularly reviewing your credit report ensures its accuracy and helps you take control of your financial health.

Mindset Matters

When reviewing your credit report, focus on two key questions:

1. **Accuracy**: Is the information correct?

2. **Ownership**: Does this information pertain to you?

Approaching your credit report with this mindset helps identify errors and potential signs of identity theft.

Key Sections on Your Credit Report

While the layout may vary among the three major credit bureaus—Equifax, Experian, and TransUnion—your credit report typically comprises the following sections:

Personal Information

This section includes:

- **Names**: Current and former names, including aliases.

- **Social Security Number**: Usually, only the last four digits are displayed.

- **Date of Birth**

- **Addresses**: Current and previous residential addresses.

- **Contact Information**: Phone numbers and email addresses.

  Tip: *Ensure all personal details are accurate. Discrepancies might indicate identity theft or clerical errors.*

Employment History

List your current and past employers. While this does not affect your credit score, it is used for identity verification.

> **Watch for:** *Employers you don't recognize, which could signal identity theft.*

Credit Accounts

This is the most detailed section, encompassing:

- **Account Types**: Credit cards, mortgages, auto loans, student loans, etc.

- **Account Status**: Open, closed, paid, charged-off, etc.

- **Payment History**: On-time payments, late payments, defaults.

- **Credit Limits and Loan Amounts**: Original and current balances.

- **Dates**: When accounts were opened or closed.

Don't Forget the Key Factors Influencing Your FICO Score:

- **Payment History**: 35%

- **Amounts Owed (Credit Utilization)**: 30%

- **Length of Credit History**: 15%

- **New Credit**: 10%

- **Credit Mix**: 10%

> **Note:** *Maintaining low credit utilization (preferably below 30%) and making timely payments are crucial for a healthy credit score.*

1. Public Records

Currently, the only public records included in credit reports are bankruptcies. While tax liens and civil judgments are not present in your credit reports, they may still exist in public records.

Bankruptcy Reporting Duration:

Chapter 7: Remains for 10 years.

Chapter 13: Remains for 7 years.

> **Action Step**: *If you find outdated or incorrect public records, dispute them promptly.*

2. Credit Inquiries

Reflects who has accessed your credit report:

- **Soft inquiries** occur when you check your own credit or when lenders preapprove offers; these do not affect your credit score.

- **Hard Inquiries**: Occur when you apply for credit. These can slightly lower your credit score and remain on your report for two years.

Tip: Multiple hard inquiries in a short period can impact your score. However, credit scoring models often treat multiple inquiries for the same type of loan (e.g., mortgage, auto) within a 45-day window as a single inquiry.

Identifying and Addressing Errors

Regularly reviewing your credit report helps spot inaccuracies, such as:

- Accounts you didn't open.

- Incorrect payment histories.

- Duplicate accounts.

- Wrong account statuses.

Steps to Dispute Errors:

1. **Gather Documentation**: Collect evidence supporting your claim.

2. **Contact the Credit Bureau:**

    - **Equifax**: www.equifax.com

    - **Experian**: www.experian.com/disputes

    - **TransUnion**: www.transunion.com/credit-disputes

3. **By mail or over the phone: dispute by mail or over the phone.**

    - **Equifax:** You can dispute online or by mail to Equifax Information Services, LLC, P.O. Box 740256, Atlanta, GA 30374-0256. Dispute over the phone at (866) 349-5191.

    - **Experian:** You can dispute information online or over the phone using the tollfree number included on your credit report. Dispute by mail at Experian, P.O. Box 4500, Allen, TX 75013.

    - **TransUnion:** Call the toll-free number (800) 916-8800, dispute online or by mail to TransUnion Consumer Solutions, P.O. Box 2000, Chester, PA, 190162000. Make sure to complete and include the request form on the website.

4. **Submit a Dispute**: Clearly identify the error, provide supporting documents, and request a correction.

5. **Follow Up**: The bureau typically investigates within 30 days. They will inform you of the outcome and provide a free copy of your updated report if changes are made.

Note: *Disputing online is convenient, but sending disputes via certified mail provides a paper trail.*

Obtaining Your Free Credit Reports

You're entitled to one free credit report every 12 months from each of the three major bureaus. Access them at AnnualCreditReport.com.

Strategy: *Stagger your requests (e.g., one every four months) to track your credit throughout the year.*

Chapter 10
Are You Really Ready for Credit?

You've probably heard all kinds of opinions about credit. Some people treat it like a financial blessing. Others call it a trap. The truth? Both views can be valid.

If you're not ready to handle credit responsibly, then yes, you *should* avoid it like the plague. But if you can manage it wisely, credit doesn't have to be the villain in your story. In fact, it can be one of your strongest financial tools.

Credit is a tool. In the right hands, it builds. In the wrong hands, it buries.

Your credit score works like your financial résumé. If you've never worked anywhere, an employer wouldn't have much to evaluate. Credit works the same way. Without a history, lenders have no way to assess whether you're likely to pay them back. And when lenders don't have enough information, they do what anyone would do—they protect themselves by increasing your interest rates or requiring larger security deposits.

The higher your score, the lower your cost of borrowing.

And let's be clear: no credit or poor credit can cost you. It can make renting a home more expensive, make buying a car harder, and even increase your insurance premiums. But before you jump into credit-building, ask yourself this: *Are you financially and emotionally ready to handle it?*

According to the latest data from the **New York Federal Reserve**, **consumer debt now exceeds $18.04 trillion**, and **the average credit card balance is nearly $6,800 per household**. These aren't just numbers—they reflect habits, stress, and sometimes avoidable financial pain.

Just because you qualify for credit doesn't mean you're ready for it. You don't want to be the "average household" buried in debt—you want to be the responsible anomaly.

I've had credit cards, and I've had credit card debt, too. I'll talk more about that in a future lesson, but here's what I've learned along the way:

> **Use credit as a stepping stone, not a stumbling block.**

If you're still unsure whether you're ready, the quick quiz below can help you get a clearer picture.

Check Yourself: Are YOU Ready for Credit?

1. How are you at saving money?

    a. Great

    b. Needs improvement

    c. I don't feel like I have any money to save

2. What kind of shopper are you?

    a. I think before I make a purchase

    b. I shop according to my mood

    c. I make knee-jerk spending decisions

3. What does interest mean when *you* borrow money?

    a. Extra money you have to pay back on top of what you borrowed

    b. A reward the bank gives you for using a credit card

4. Do you have an emergency fund?

    a. Yes

    b. No

5. Making a payment one day late is not a big deal.

    a. True

    b. False

6. I should use my credit card for everyday expenses when I'm broke.

    a. True

    b. False

7. Carrying a balance on my credit card is a good thing.

    a. True

    b. False

8. Do you regularly track your income and expenses?

    a. Yes, I use a budget or app

    b. Sometimes, but I could be more consistent

    c. No, I just try to keep up mentally

9. How do you handle financial setbacks?

a. I tap into savings or an emergency fund

b. I put it on a credit card and hope for the best

c. I avoid dealing with it until it becomes urgent

10. Why do you want a credit card?

a. To build credit and learn money management

b. For rewards and convenience

c. Because I feel like I need one to get by

Answer Key & Reflection

While this isn't a pass-or-fail quiz, here's how to interpret your answers:

- **Mostly A's**: You're on the right track. You have the habits and mindset to start building credit responsibly.

- **Mostly B's**: You're aware but inconsistent. It might be helpful to build more structure into your financial habits before diving into credit.

- **Mostly C's**: You may want to work on your money management skills before applying for credit. Consider starting with a budgeting system, building an emergency fund, or seeking guidance first.

Final Thought:

Credit doesn't have to define you, but how you use it absolutely will. The best time to build healthy habits is *before* you need them.

FYI: If you find yourself overwhelmed by debt. Consider This Before You File for Bankruptcy

If you feel like you're drowning in debt, and someone is in your ear—or it's crossed your mind—that bankruptcy is the *only* way out, let's have a real conversation.

> **Bankruptcy is not your only option.**
>
> **It may be the best choice for some individuals, depending on their circumstances, but it should never be the first or sole solution you consider.**

I say this from personal experience.

In my twenties, I filed for bankruptcy because I was $16,000 in debt, mostly from credit cards and a bad car loan. At the time, I didn't know there were other options. I just knew I needed relief. Looking back, I wish someone had told me there were other paths I could have tried first.

(That's also why you must be careful who you share your money struggles with. Sometimes it's the blind leading the blind, and their advice, though well-meaning, can cost you in the long run.)

If I had known what I know now, I would have contacted my credit card companies and the car loan lender *before* things got too far. Many companies are willing to work with you if you explain what's going on—whether it's a job loss, an illness, or simply being behind. You can often negotiate lower payments, temporary pauses, or even debt forgiveness.

But you have more power when you're proactive. **Ignoring the problem only limits your choices.**

Bankruptcy should be a last resort, not a first step.

And truth be told, it wasn't as easy or private as I thought it would be. It cost me over $1,000 just to file—money I had to borrow. My filing was even printed in the local newspaper. (I'm not sure if they still do that, but when I filed, they did.) It was a tough season.

I'm not sharing this to shame anyone. I'm sharing this because I wish someone had told me this before I made that decision.

There are options. But you have to know what questions to ask.

Ask Yourself These Questions Before You File for Bankruptcy:

1. **Have I talked to a nonprofit credit counselor about my situation?**

   They can often help you make a plan, and it's usually free or low-cost.

2. **Have I contacted my creditors to see if they can negotiate or settle?**

   You might be surprised by their flexibility once you reach out.

3. **Is most of my debt unsecured (like credit cards), or do I have assets that could be sold or refinanced instead?**

4. **Do I understand how bankruptcy will affect my credit score, future purchases, and financial goals?**

   Some things stay on your credit report for up to 10 years.

5. **Am I filing because I feel hopeless, or because I've exhausted every other option?**

   Sometimes the pressure makes us want a quick escape, but long-term relief may require a little more patience.

You deserve peace of mind, not just relief from debt.

So, take your time, ask questions, and remember: **bankruptcy is one option, but it's not the only one.**

Real-World Inspiration: Tiffany "The Budgetnista" Aliche

One of the most inspiring credit recovery stories that has truly resonated with me on my financial journey is that of Tiffany Aliche, known as The Budgetnista. Imagine facing the harsh reality of losing your job during the 2008 recession—an experience that many can relate to. Tiffany fell behind on her bills, lost her home, and faced the daunting challenge of damaged credit.

It's easy to feel overwhelmed in such circumstances, but Tiffany chose not to stay stuck in her situation. Instead, she picked herself up, rebuilt her credit, and transformed her hardships into a powerful teaching tool for others.

Her journey is a profound reminder that our past does not dictate our financial future. If she can rise from such difficulties, so can we Tiffany's experience encourages us all to believe in our ability to turn obstacles into opportunities. Remember, your story may one day inspire someone else. No matter where you are right now, hold on to hope and take those steps forward, you have the strength to create a brighter financial future Her story and mine are proof that your past does not define your financial future, and you will be that example for someone one day, too.

THE MOMENTUM

Keep going. It is not about perfection; it is about progress.

Chapter 11

Understanding Secured
vs.
Unsecured Credit Cards Confidently

Credit is one of the most misunderstood tools in your financial toolbox. It can either open doors to opportunity or block you if you don't use it wisely. But here's the truth: credit isn't the enemy. Confusion, avoidance, and poor planning are. Let's discuss how to use credit with confidence, starting with one of the most common questions: **What's the difference between secured and unsecured credit cards?**

Secured Credit Cards

If you're still a little anxious about handling credit, a secured credit card is one way to ease your nerves. The only thing at risk is your own money.

A secured credit card requires a cash deposit that acts as your credit limit. For example, if you deposit $500, your spending limit will be $500. These cards are easier to qualify for than unsecured credit cards and are a great tool for building or rebuilding credit.

My Story: I didn't start with a secured credit card, but I did have to rebuild my credit after a few missteps in my 20s. I honestly don't even remember the name of the card issuer now, but I do remember how it felt when I got approved for a small unsecured limit—maybe around $500. After using it wisely for about 12 months, I was offered a credit limit increase, and eventually, my credit card was upgraded without needing a deposit.

Today, many lenders still offer a similar path: if you manage your secured card responsibly, you may get your deposit returned and be upgraded to an unsecured card.

Key Tips When Choosing a Secured Credit Card:
- Look for lenders who report to all **three major credit bureaus** (Equifax, TransUnion, Experian).
- Choose a lender that offers a **path to upgrade** to an unsecured card.
- Watch out for **high annual fees** or hidden charges.
- Make sure your payment history is actually being reported—otherwise, it won't help your credit.

Unsecured Credit Cards

An unsecured credit card is what most people think of when they hear "credit card." No deposit is required because the lender is taking on more risk. Instead, your approval and credit limit are based on your credit history and score.

You will still have a credit limit, interest on unpaid balances, and minimum monthly payments. These cards are ideal if you already have a decent credit score or a history of on- time payments.

5 Steps to Choosing Your First Credit Card:

- **Identify Your Why.** Why do you want a credit card? Is it to build credit, prepare for emergencies, or earn rewards?

- **Do Your Research.** Read the fine print. Look for interest rates, annual fees, and penalties for late payments.

- **Have Consistent Income.** If you're going to create a bill, make sure you can pay it.

- **Consider Becoming an Authorized User.** If starting from scratch feels overwhelming, ask a parent or trusted adult if you can become an authorized user on their card. *(I did this for my son to help him establish credit the smart way.)*

- **Use It Responsibly.** Becoming an authorized user allows you to build credit without taking on full responsibility.

Quick Comparison Chart

Features	Secured Credit Card	Unsecured Credit Card
Requires Deposit	Yes	No
Easier to Get Approved?	Yes	Depends on credit score
Builds Credit?	Yes	Yes
Reports to Credit Bureaus?	Yes	Yes
Ideal For	New or rebuilding credit	Established credit history
Can Be Upgraded?	Often, after 6–12 months	Not applicable

Mini Confidence Checklist

Before applying for any credit card, ask yourself:

- Is the card issuer reputable?

- Are they reporting to all three major credit bureaus?

- What are the fees, interest rates, and terms?

- Is this card helping me reach a specific financial goal?

Final Thoughts

Whether you're just starting your credit journey or repairing your credit after a few financial plot twists, remember **you can do this**. Your credit score is not a moral compass; it's a learning tool. You are not your past mistakes. You're your next decision.

Let credit work for you, not against you. And no matter where you are in your journey, keep going. Because financial confidence starts with just one informed decision at a time.

Chapter 12

How to Avoid Credit Card Debt

| "Don't let your swipe today become your stress tomorrow."

As stated in an earlier chapter, the average American household carries nearly $6,800 in credit card debt. Needless to say, many cardholders aren't using credit responsibly.

Experience was my teacher when it came to credit card debt, but feel free to learn from my mistakes so you won't have to repeat them.

Credit card debt is heavy. It not only weighs on your wallet, but it can also rob you of peace, rest, and choices. You might even find yourself lying awake, wondering how it all added up so quickly. (Or was that just me?)

Memories of vacations you've enjoyed or the joy in your child's eyes on Christmas morning after you used your credit card to be a generous Santa are priceless. But the bill that arrives in January cannot be paid with memories.

Memories are priceless, but you cannot pay the credit card bill with them.

Getting into credit card debt is a lot like gaining weight—it sneaks up on you. And most of the time, the ride to debt feels like freedom, until reality shows up with the invoice.

If you've ever used a credit card to bridge the gap between paychecks, splurge during birthdays, or chase a feeling during a rough season, you're not alone. I've done all of that too.

As a single mom, I often felt intensified guilt. I wanted my son to feel secure and to have everything he needed—even when extras were beyond my budget. At times, I purchased items out of love, and at other times, out of a sense of shame.

Over the years, I've helped others who found themselves buried in credit card debt for various reasons: covering medical bills, job loss, business ventures, or even unexpected funerals. So many of these reasons come from a place of survival, not recklessness.

But regardless of how it starts, credit card debt is easy to accumulate and hard to escape. That's why this chapter exists.

Let's talk about how to *avoid* it.

Understand How Credit Card Companies Make Their Money

Before we break the cycle, we need to know how the system works. Once you understand how credit card companies make a profit, you can stop unknowingly helping them at your expense.

Interest Charges

Carrying a balance each month triggers interest. The average rate is around **21.91%**. That means if you owe $1,000 and only pay the minimum, you're handing over hundreds more just in interest over time.

> **Tip:** *Always aim to pay your balance in full to avoid interest altogether.*

Late Fees

If you pay even *one* day late, you'll be charged. According to WalletHub, the average late fee is **$30.50**, and repeated late payments could result in charges of up to **$40** per occurrence, as well as a drop in your credit score.

> **Tip:** *Automate your payments or set calendar reminders so you never miss a due date.*

Cash Advance Fees

Cash advances are one of the most expensive forms of borrowing. Not only do you lose your grace period, but interest starts accruing *immediately,* often at rates from **24.99% to 29.99%**.

> **"A cash advance may feel like a lifeline, but it comes with chains."**

> **Tip:** *Always explore every other option first. These fees are designed to capitalize on your desperation.*

Balance Transfer Fees

Transferring a balance can be a smart debt-payoff move—*if* you do the math first. Most cards charge **3%–5%** of the amount you're transferring.

Example: Transferring $2,000 at 3% costs $60. At 5%, it's $100.

> **Tip:** *Look for 0% APR introductory offers and weigh whether the savings outweigh the transfer fee.*

Annual Fees

Some cards charge you simply for having them. Unless you're getting significant rewards or perks, it's not worth it.

> **Tip:** *Choose cards without annual fees—especially if you're rebuilding credit. When your score improves, graduate to a no-fee card.*

Miscellaneous Fees

- **Foreign Transaction Fees:** Up to 3% for using your card internationally.

- **Interchange Fees:** These are charged to merchants (1%–3%) and are why some stores offer cash discounts.

Visual Breakdown: How Credit Card Companies Make Profits

Fee Type	Description	Average Cost/Rate
Interest Charges	Ongoing charges on unpaid balances	~21.91%
Late Fees	Penalty for missing due dates	$30.50 to $40
Cash Advance Fees	Immediate high-interest borrowing	24.99%–29.99% + flat fee
Balance Transfer Fee	Cost to move debt to a new card	3%–5% of balance
Annual Fees	Yearly charge just to use the card	$69 (avg for low-tier cards)
Foreign Transaction	Charge for overseas use	Up to 3%

How Long it Takes to Pay Off Credit Card Debt If You Only Make the Minimum Payment

Assume a credit card balance of **$3,000** at **21% APR**, with a **2% minimum monthly payment**:

Minimum Payment Plan	Time to Pay Off	Total Interest Paid	Total Paid
Only Minimum Payments	~17 years	Over $4,700	Over $7,700
$100/month	~4 years	Around $1,000	Around $4,000
$200/month	~1.5 years	Less than $500	Around $3,500

This chart is a powerful reminder: even a few extra dollars each month can save you years of payments and thousands in interest.

How to Avoid the Credit Card Debt Traps

Here's how to be intentional without living in fear:

- **Treat credit cards like debit cards.** Only spend what you can pay off in full each month.

- **Use a budget.** A realistic one. Account for birthdays, holidays, and random expenses.

- **Avoid carrying balances.** If you *must* carry a balance, create a repayment plan.

- **Keep your credit utilization low.** Aim to use less than 30% of your available credit.

- **Don't open store cards just for the discount.** Most of them have high interest and low limits.

- **Say no to cash advances.** It's expensive and rarely worth it.

- **Negotiate interest rates.** Call your issuer and ask for a lower rate—they may say yes.

- **Automate payments.** Even just the minimum to avoid late fees.

> "Avoiding credit card debt isn't about having more money—it's about making fewer costly decisions."

Final Words of Encouragement

Credit cards are tools, not a way of life. And like any tool, they can help or hurt depending on how you use them. This chapter isn't about shame—it's about strategy.

You're not behind. You're just getting better at being financially prepared. You're making smarter choices, asking the right questions, and starting to think like someone who's building financial freedom—not just surviving paycheck to paycheck.

> Credit cards don't cause debt—decisions do.

Keep showing up for your future. You're worth every ounce of effort you're putting in.

Progress isn't about perfection—it's about becoming more aware and acting on what you now know.

Chapter 13

Is It Worth It?

Let's be real—most people swipe their cards without fully understanding the long-term *cost* of that swipe. The truth? Credit card interest is **compounded daily**, not just monthly, so the longer you carry a balance, the more costly that purchase becomes.

Morgan Housel said: *"Doing well with money has a little to do with how smart you are and a lot to do with how you behave."* Let's change our behavior—beginning with awareness.

How Credit Card Interest Works

If you carry a balance month to month, your credit card interest adds up *daily*, based on your **average daily balance** and **APR** (Annual Percentage Rate). Let's walk through the real math.

If your APR is 20.87%, here's how you figure out what you're being charged:

Step 1: Convert your APR to a daily rate

- $20.87 \div 100 = 0.2087$

- $0.2087 \div 365 = 0.00057 \rightarrow$ that's your **daily rate**

Step 2: Multiply by your average daily balance

Let's say you made one $700 purchase during a 25-day billing cycle.

Your average daily balance = $700

Step 3: Calculate your interest charge

($700 x 0.00057) x 25 = **$9.98**

So that $700 purchase cost you nearly *$10 extra* if you didn't pay it off.

Smart Shortcut: There are free interest calculators on sites like NerdWallet or Experian—use them.

The Why?

| "Being average is easy Being amazing takes work "

I often say this—and when it comes to credit card debt, it's particularly true. The U.S. credit card system is designed for **instant gratification**. It makes buying *easy* and paying *painful*.

Swipe first. Regret later. Sound familiar?

That's because spending on credit doesn't provide the same emotional "sting" as parting with actual money. That's why I challenge you to ask yourself...

| **Do I spend more or less when I use a credit card instead of cash?**

Me? I spend a lot less when I use cash because I have to be intentional. Even at my big age, I give myself a weekly allowance. That physical limit helps me make deliberate choices.

Additional Tips to Avoid Credit Card Debt

Here are practical (and personal) ways to avoid becoming a part of the *average* debt statistic:

1. Build an Emergency Fund

Even Dave Ramsey got this one right. $1,000 is a great starting goal—but even $100 to $200 can save you from swiping your credit card when life throws a curveball.

| **"Use credit for convenience, not for survival."**

If you can't afford to pay off a purchase in full when the bill arrives, you can't afford it.

2. Live Below Your Means

A simple truth: financial peace doesn't come from income—it comes from habits.

One of the most powerful lessons I learned was this:

| **Retirement is more about a financial number than a physical age**

If you avoid credit card debt, invest wisely, and build effective habits, you can achieve your financial goals without waiting until you're 67. This begins with living slightly below your means now.

3. Don't Buy Things You Can't Afford

It's worth repeating. Here's how I break impulsive spending habits for myself and others:

Calculate your time cost:

If you make $25/hour and want something that costs $200, that's 8 hours of work.

Ask yourself: *Is it worth 8 hours of my life?*

Even if you're salaried, break it down. You'll think differently.

4. Keep Your Minimum Payment at $0

If your **minimum payment is $0**, you have no balance, and that's how you avoid debt traps: Pay it in full and start each month fresh.

5. Know When to Say When

You don't need five credit cards. More cards mean more temptation and more to manage. Stick to one or two.

6. Stick to Your Budget

This sounds basic, but it's not always easy. Set a budget that reflects your *goals*, not your impulses. Review it often, especially when your income or expenses shift.

7. Practice Financial Patience

Save for big purchases. Delay the "buy" until you've got the funds. That's a flex most people aren't disciplined enough to do—but you're not most people.

8. Avoid Cash Advances

Unless it's a true emergency and you have no other option, **don't** use your credit card like an ATM. Interest rates on cash advances are higher, and they usually start charging immediately.

Final Thoughts

We don't talk enough about how credit card debt is often emotional—not logical. Sometimes we spend because we're stressed, comparing, bored, or trying to fill a void.

Morgan Housel, author of The Psychology of Money, said: *"Saving money is the gap between your ego and your income."*

You don't have to prove anything to anybody. Keep your peace. Protect your future.

Now, here's a **5-question quiz** you can use to commit this to memory:

Avoiding Credit Card Debt

What does it mean if your minimum credit card payment is $0.00?

A. You're late on your payment
B. You owe interest
C. **You've paid off your balance in full**
D. You've exceeded your limit

What is a major reason people accumulate credit card debt, according to this section?

A. **They forget to use coupons**
B. **They only use cash**
C. **Instant gratification and impulse spending**
D. **They close all credit accounts**

What's one benefit of living below your financial means?

A. You'll qualify for fewer rewards programs
B. **You can save for retirement and emergencies**
C. You won't get approved for loans
D. It guarantees wealth

What is the financial patience strategy used to avoid debt?

A. Asking a friend to co-sign
B. **Saving for large purchases over time**
C. Borrowing from family
D. Waiting for store credit offers

Why is calculating how many hours you'd need to work to buy something useful?

A. It helps you guess your paycheck
B. It makes shopping more fun
C. **It builds awareness about your spending habits**
D. It lowers the item's price

Chapter 14

Why Credit Still Matters —
Even When It Feels Like It Shouldn't

Let's have some real hard conversations: building credit can feel like a game designed for you to lose. One missed payment, one unexpected bill, or simply not fully understanding how the system works can lead to your score suffering the consequences. It's frustrating, and quite honestly, it's not fair. Believe me when I say that you are not the only one who feels this way.

But here's the financial truth: credit still matters even though the system is flawed. Even when it's hard to trust, even when you're doing your best and it doesn't seem to be enough, credit continues to loom in the background of some of life's biggest decisions. I know how frustrating credit can be, but it is also necessary.

> **Credit Impacts Where You Live. Whether renting your first place or trying to move into a better neighborhood, your credit gets checked. Landlords use it to decide whether to rent to you and how much to charge for a deposit. Sometimes the reasons are valid; other times they are convenient.**

Over 20 years ago, after relocating to the East Coast, I encountered a housing gatekeeping moment I'll never forget. Despite meeting every listed qualification, a rental agent discouraged me from applying, citing new, unclear policies and steep, non- refundable background check costs. The tone, the probing, the microaggressions—were all too real. I didn't know my rights then, so I allowed her to talk me out of applying. But the silver lining? That experience planted the seed for my career in helping Veterans secure housing and understand their renter rights.

Financial bottom line: Never let something you can control—like your credit score— stand between you and the life you want to build.

If you'd like to understand your Fair Housing and rental rights, start here: <u>Fair Housing</u>.

> **Credit Affects How You Get Around. Most dealerships check credit for car loans, even for used cars. Poor credit can lead to higher rates, increased payments, or possibly no loan at all.**

At one point, my credit was so poor that even a co-signer couldn't help me. I'll never forget the humiliation of being told my name couldn't appear on a loan. My grandmother, who couldn't even drive, believed in me enough to take out the loan herself. Thanks to her excellent credit, I received a great interest rate. I paid extra every month to show her that her trust in me wasn't misplaced. That experience taught me two lessons: protect those who protect you—and that no one should ever be able to tell you your name isn't good enough.

Today? My credit is exceptional. And even though I know cars depreciate quickly, the freedom of choice is a blessing I've earned.

> **Credit Makes Homeownership Possible. Homeownership remains one of the most powerful ways to build generational wealth in America. But good credit is the gatekeeper.**

A credit score 620 might get you in the door, but it will literally cost you. According to Experian, borrowers with scores in the very good (740-799) or exceptional (800-850) range can save tens of thousands over the life of a loan compared to someone barely meeting the minimum.

> **Credit Helps Build Something Bigger. Whether you dream of owning a business, launching a side hustle, or scaling your passion project, credit can be the key to accessing the resources you need.**

As someone with a full-time job and entrepreneurial ventures on the side, I'm grateful that my business revenue often gets reinvested right back in. However, invoices can take 90-100 days to get paid, and those gaps can be brutal. Good credit bridges that gap. It keeps the lights on when cash flow is slow, allowing me to cover LLC fees and quarterly taxes and keep everything afloat.

> **Credit Can Affect Jobs and Opportunities. Some employers check your credit, especially in roles tied to finances or requiring security clearances.**

They can't see your score, but they receive a modified version of your credit report, which includes payment history, bankruptcies, liens, and sometimes even employment history. It's legal. It's flawed. But it's still real.

> **Credit Provides a Backup Plan. Life is unpredictable. Unexpected travel, medical bills, car repairs—things happen. When used responsibly, credit can serve as your emergency backup.**

I've used credit cards in emergencies rather than pulling from savings. Why? Because if I can pay it off by the next billing cycle, it's essentially a short-term, interest-free loan. That way, my plot twist fund stays untouched for the real "in-case-of-fire" moments.

The Financial Bottom Line

Your credit is not your character. But it is a tool—and when used wisely, it can create freedom, choice, and access. I get it. The system is frustrating, and it hasn't always been fair. That's why you don't improve your credit for bragging rights—you do it for freedom. The freedom to live where you want. Drive what you need. Build what you believe in. So, that means you don't get to throw in the towel. It means you get smarter, stronger, and more strategic.

Your story doesn't end with rejection. It begins with you reclaiming your power—and building the kind of credit that doesn't just open doors but keeps them open. Because when life happens, and it will, your credit can be the quiet strength that helps you stay on your feet—and move forward on your terms.

More Financial Realities:

- **Nearly 1 in 3 Americans** have a credit score below 601, considered "poor," but credit scores are not permanent. (Source: Experian)
- A person with a **760 credit score can save over $80,000** in interest on a 30-year mortgage compared to someone with a 620 score. (Source: CNBC)
- **43% of landlords** run credit checks during rental applications. (Source: TransUnion)
- **60% of employers** run some form of background check that may include a credit check. (Source: SHRM)

FINANCIAL BONUS GEMS

Consistency is key

Chapter 15

Student Loans –
A Decision That Lasts Decades

Quote to remember:

"Student loans are the only thing that's so easy to get—and so hard to get rid of."

Dave Ramsey

According to the U.S. Department of Education, 42.7 million people in the United States hold student loan debt, totaling over $1.6 trillion.

If you haven't borrowed yet, do everything you can to keep it that way. If you already have, don't panic—but be proactive instead.

Student loan debt can follow you for decades. Unfortunately, many borrowers don't fully understand the long-term financial commitment they're making when they take out student loans. I know I didn't. I only knew I wanted to go to college, and student loans seemed like the way to get there. I wish I had taken the time to ask more questions.

Moment of Financial Clarity: Exercise caution with loans that are easily accessible to most borrowers, and be especially wary of loans that cannot be discharged through bankruptcy. This is not an advantage—it's a warning sign.

Student loan debt jeopardizes your wages, tax returns, and retirement. Therefore, before you sign anything, consider this: is the risk truly worth the reward?

If you already have student loan debt, ignoring it won't make it go away. In fact, the consequences can be long-lasting and expensive. Student loans can negatively impact your credit score, increase your debt-to-income ratio, and limit your financial freedom.

Here's what happens if you miss a payment:

- The day after your payment is due, your loan is considered *delinquent*.
- After 90 days, that delinquency is reported to the national credit bureaus.
- If the delinquency continues, your loan will go into *default*.

And once your loan is in default:

- You're no longer eligible for deferment or forbearance.
- You won't qualify for federal student aid (like Pell Grants).

- Your school might withhold your transcripts.
- Your wages or tax refunds may be garnished.

Let's pause and define two important terms:

Student Loan Deferment allows you to temporarily stop making payments on your federal student loans under specific conditions, such as if you are in school, unemployed, or facing financial hardship. Interest may still accrue depending on the loan type. Learn more at Federal Student Aid - Deferment.

Student Loan Forbearance is another temporary pause or reduction in your loan payments, often granted during financial hardship or illness. Unlike deferment, interest almost always accrues during forbearance. Read more at Federal Student Aid - Forbearance.

Moment of Financial Clarity: Student loans are one of the few debts that can't be discharged in bankruptcy. That makes them very different from other types of borrowing. Think long and hard about that before committing.

If you don't know who your student loan servicer is, contact the Federal Student Aid Information Center at 1-800-433-3243 or visit studentaid.gov.

Speaking from experience, I only used student loans for my bachelor's degree. The military covered my MBA. Thankfully, because I work for a nonprofit through the SSVF Program, I was eligible for the Public Service Loan Forgiveness (PSLF) Program. After 120 qualifying payments, the rest of my student loan balance was forgiven. That took nearly a decade, but it was worth it.

Still, I would have done things differently if I could go back. I would have applied for more scholarships and grants. I would have considered work-study programs, on-campus jobs, employer tuition assistance, and any other option that didn't involve borrowing. I didn't know back then that searching for free money should be treated like a part-time job. Now you do.

To learn more about free money for college, visit the Federal Student Aid website.

MyScholly.com is another excellent scholarship resource, so feel free to start your search there too.

What is a Pell Grant?

A Pell Grant is free money from the federal government for undergraduate students who demonstrate financial need. You don't repay a Pell Grant. You apply by completing the FAFSA—the Free Application for Federal Student Aid.

Closing financial thoughts:

If you're thinking about student loans, stop and do the math. Explore every alternative. Ask every question. Student loans might seem like the answer today, but they could limit your choices tomorrow. The goal is not just to go to college—it's to graduate without being buried in debt. That starts with making smarter decisions now.

Chapter 16

Homeownership Isn't the Dream—
It's a Strategy

| Sometimes the key to generational wealth isn't glamor—it's stability.

I know owning a home is still considered a major part of the "American Dream." But honestly? It depends on who you ask and what season of life they're in.

Let me be real with you—when I bought my home, it wasn't because I was trying to check off a box on the American Dream bucket list. I simply needed more space. I had outgrown the townhouse I was renting, and when I started looking at larger rentals closer to my job and the expressway, the prices were... ridiculous. I mean, $700 more a month for just *one* extra room. And on top of that, the rent increased yearly with no upgrades or improvements to justify it.

So yes, I made a quick decision. It boiled down to this: continue feeling cramped and uncomfortable, or determine what it would take to own something that made financial and spatial sense. The interest rates at the time were reasonable, so I crunched the numbers, checked what I could afford, and began the pre-approval process.

But I'll admit, part of the delay in buying sooner came from all the noise around me.

> "Wait until you're married."
>
> "You should have 20 saved for a down payment."
>
> "Being responsible for repairs is too much—just keep renting."

Let me share this from personal experience: **don't let someone else's fear or limitations hold you back or make you doubt your faith.** Homeownership may not be right for them, but that doesn't affect you. You've got to trust *your* instincts and *your* timing.

Real estate is a financial decision, not a fairytale.

Homeownership can be a solid investment, but it's also one of the biggest and longest financial commitments you'll ever make. That's why you've got to do your homework and get clear on your "why." Like everything else in life, **it starts with why.**

Once you've defined your why, ask yourself these four questions:

1. Are you financially ready?

And not just "ready to move out." I mean, do you have a stable income? Manageable debt? Decent credit? Homeownership is a long-term relationship with your finances— don't rush into it without doing a full financial self-check.

2. Can you make a respectable down payment?

Don't get hung up on the mythical 20%. I didn't even put that much down—I'm a veteran, so I had different options. But you *will* need to put down something, and you'll want to have closing costs and emergency savings too.

3. Can you afford the monthly payment and the extras?

Your mortgage might be cheaper than rent, depending on where you live. That was my situation on the East Coast. But remember, owning means paying for things your landlord used to cover— like water, sewer, HOA fees, trash pickup, and all those random home expenses no one tells you about until they hit your bank account.

4. Are you good with tools, or at least YouTube?

Once you're the owner, you can no longer call maintenance. That leaky faucet or clogged toilet is *your* problem. I recommend purchasing a home warranty for major repairs and for the minor stuff. YouTube University has saved me more than once. (Shoutout to the video that taught me how to change a flapper valve on a toilet and air filters.)

If you answered "yes" to all four questions, you're ready to take the next step. I highly recommend signing up for a **free first-time homebuyer's workshop** in your area. It'll help you understand the full process—budgeting, inspections, and closing.

Moment of Financial Clarity:

Your first home is just that—your *first* home. It likely won't be your last. So don't stretch yourself so thin trying to get the biggest house you can. Be intentional and stay well below your pre-approval amount if possible. I bought a home nearly 30% below what I qualified for, and that gave me breathing room for savings, travel, and a "plot twist" repair fund. *Start with the one you need, not the one of your dreams.*

Yes, the market has shifted. Interest rates are higher. Inventory is low. Prices have climbed. But that doesn't mean the door is closed—it just means you need to approach it with strategy instead of sentiment.

Final Thought:

Owning a home isn't the end goal—it's one of the tools. One that can offer you tax breaks, equity, stability, and something solid to pass down. Remember: you're not chasing a dream... you're building a foundation.

EPILOGUE OF ENCOURAGEMENT

This may be the final page of the workbook, but your journey doesn't end here. And before you close this book for good, I want you to hear me clearly: **you are more than capable of doing everything you just read — and more.**

Yes, this is the end of the workbook, but don't forget the beginning. Remember when I shared that my credit score was once a 450? That wasn't the end of my story — it was the start of a new one. And if you're in a similar situation right now, I want you to know that **you have the tools and the power to rewrite your financial story.**

Will it take time? Absolutely. Will it require patience and sacrifice? Without a doubt. But the change you're working toward is possible — and it's worth it.

When your waiting season ends, the 800 club will await you. Until then, lean into this new mindset, keep using the tools you've picked up, and stay consistent.

Consistency is the real key.

It builds momentum, creates progress, and requires a daily commitment to the version of yourself that you're striving to become. Remember that meaningful change doesn't occur overnight in a world that moves at the speed of a scroll. Financial goals, like any life goals, need time, intention, and a few necessary sacrifices.

That may look like skipping a few games, happy hours, brunches, pausing subscriptions, or trading your favorite show for some quality time with your budget. And while that might feel uncomfortable at first, that discomfort is a sign that you're growing.

Mistakes will happen. You might fall off track. But here's the truth: **mistakes mature into mastery, even financial ones.** You don't have to be perfect. You have to be committed. The very first thing—the most important thing—that you can do right now (and it costs nothing) is **to believe that you can achieve this.**

I'm proud of you for making it this far. Keep going. You've got this.

If you ever wish to share your progress, have a question, or need a bit of motivation, just send me a message. You can connect with me on social media at @AmazingChapters on Instagram or email me at Beamazing@dontforgetu.com.

I'll be cheering for you every step of the way.

Take care and don't forget to be amazing,

Xoxo LaShon

Suggested Reading Materials

The One Week Budget by Tiffany Aliche

A simple and empowering guide to creating a money system in just seven days— perfect for beginners looking to take control of their finances quickly.

Get Good with Money by Tiffany Aliche

Ten practical steps to becoming financially whole—this book breaks down budgeting, saving, investing, and more with real-life strategies.

The Psychology of Money by Morgan Housel

A powerful reminder that how we *think* about money often matters more than how much we know—timeless lessons on behavior, mindset, and decisions.

The Total Money Makeover by Dave Ramsey

A no-fluff plan to pay off debt, build savings, and take back financial control, using Ramsey's proven, step-by-step method.

Rich Dad, Poor Dad by Robert Kiyosaki

A classic that shifts how you think about money, investing, and earning—told through the author's story of growing up with two contrasting financial role models.

The Wealth Choice by Dennis Kimbro

Based on years of interviews with successful Black millionaires, this book reveal the habits, mindset, and discipline behind generational wealth.

Mindset

Winning the War in Your Mind by Craig Groeschel

Learn how to stop believing the lies that hold you back and start rewiring your thoughts toward truth, purpose, and peace.

The Four Agreements by Don Miguel Ruiz

A spiritual and practical guide rooted in ancient wisdom—these four principles can transform how you think, speak, and live.

Personal Growth & Accountability

The Mountain Is You by Brianna Wiest

A deep dive into self-sabotage—why we do it, and how to replace it with healing, growth, and resilience.

Don't Forget To Be Amazing This Year by LaShon Fryer

A personal and powerful guide to staying accountable, showing up for yourself, and remembering your brilliance all year long.

REFERENCES AND RESOURCES

Citi. *What is a credit report and what information does it include?*

https://www.citi.com/credit-cards/understanding-credit-cards/what-is-a-credit-report

Credit Karma. *How to dispute an error on your credit report*

https://www.creditkarma.com/credit/i/dispute-error-credit-report

CreditCards.com.

https://www.creditcards.com/credit-card-news

https://www.creditcards.com/credit-card-news/rate-report/

Credit.com

www.credit.com

Financial Consumer Agency of Canada. *Financial Stress and Its Impacts*

https://www.canada.ca/en/financial-consumer-agency/services/financial-wellness-work/stress-impacts.html

Financial scarcity and cognitive performance: A meta-analysis

https://www.sciencedirect.com/science/article/pii/S0167487024000102

Federal Reserve. *Average Interchange Fee – Regulation II*

https://www.federalreserve.gov/paymentsystems/regii-average-interchange-fee.htm

Housel, M. (2020). *The Psychology of Money: Timeless Lessons on Wealth, Greed, and Happiness.* Harriman House.

Marmot Library Network.

Mindset. *Cambridge Dictionary*

https://dictionary.cambridge.org/us/dictionary/english/mindset

NerdWallet.

https://www.nerdwallet.com/article/finance/2024-financial-angst-report
https://www.nerdwallet.com/article/credit-cards/ready-first-credit-card
https://www.nerdwallet.com/blog/loans/student-loans/2018-fafsa-pell-grant/

Sinek, S. (2011). *Start with Why: How Great Leaders Inspire Everyone to Take Action*. Penguin Books.

Spent Movie.

      http://www.spentmovie.com/index.html

StudentAid.gov

      https://studentaid.gov/understand-aid/types/grants/pell

      https://studentaid.gov/h/apply-for-aid/fafsa

U.S. News. *Credit Card Fee Survey*

      https://creditcards.usnews.com/articles/fee-survey

United States Population

      https://www.worldometers.info/world-population/us-population/

CNBC.

      https://www.cnbc.com/2019/08/02/how-much-americans-earn-in-2019-compared-to-2009.html

      https://www.cnbc.com/2020/05/05/consumer-debt-hits-new-record-of-14point3-trillion.html

CardRatings. *Credit Card Interest Calculator*

      https://www.cardratings.com/credit-card-interest-calculator.html

AUTHOR INFORMATION

LaShon Fryer is a Veteran, a certified financial coach, and a nonprofit leader with an MBA and over 20 years of experience helping others achieve their goals, both financially and personally. This is her second book, written to help people confront their money stories with clarity, confidence, and no judgment. She lives and works on the East Coast, where she advocates for other Veterans by day and spoils her granddaughters in her free time when she is not assisting others with their most important project—themselves.